Old EAGLESHAM

by
Rhona Wilson

I am having a high time at Eaglesham.

By the turn of the century Eaglesham had few employment opportunities and the population fell to around the 1,000 mark, a level not seen since the eighteenth century. Ironically it was this drop which saved the village. Despite the fact that many of its buildings were dilapidated, Eaglesham had become a popular destination for Glaswegian families on holiday by the thirties. Locals were able to make money by letting out part of their homes during summer with some of the guests setting up home in the village permanently. This *c.*1910 postcard illustrates the village's commercial potential in the twentieth century, although Eaglesham was recognised as being unusually attractive even in the 1790s. The writer of the First Statistical Account stated that travellers of the time considered it to be 'one of the most delightful places in Britain'.

© 1997 Stenlake Publishing
First Published in the United Kingdom, 1997,
By Stenlake Publishing, Ochiltree Sawmill, The Lade
Ochiltree, Ayrshire, KA18 2NX
Telephone / Fax: 01290 423114

ISBN 1 84033 018 X

Eaglesham's religious history is complex, it being, at one point, very much over-populated by churches. In 1817 an unpopular choice of minister by the Earl of Eglinton led to a walk-out from the parish church. Those who left joined the Reformed Presbyterian Church and had their own building in Glendinning Place by 1825. In 1876 they merged with the Free Kirk which was set up as a result of the infamous Disruption in the early 1840s. Many churches were built in the village throughout this period resulting in a duplication of resources. Finally, in the early 1900s, the congregations of the Carswell Church and the Free Kirk were united, Carswell Church later being used as a church hall known as the Children's Church. The Parish Church standing today was built when Montgomery Street became the village Main Street. Originally a small octagonal building, it was extended at the end of the last century. The architect designed an identical church in Lochwinnoch which still stands in its original form.

Introduction

In the mid-eighteenth century the population of Eaglesham subsisted on an agricultural lifestyle unchanged for centuries. The parish was farmed on the runrig system, with strips of land worked individually and inefficiently, the tenants housed in raggle-taggle collections of farm buildings and dwellings known as fermtouns. Drainage to reclaim or improve land, the use of hedging to shelter crops, or the employment of lime and dung as fertilisers were hardly imagined. Leases for the rigs were short and, with no guarantee that he would get the same plot the following year, there was little incentive for the husbandman to make improvements. Eaglesham farmers tended to rely on the sale of dairy products to the Glasgow market, the main focus of crop cultivation beginning and ending with oats, and a hardy black-coloured variety at that. The kirkton village with its church and schoolmaster operated as an *ad hoc* service centre for the rural settlements, but one which seemed as ramshackle and impermanent as the fermtouns themselves.

When the Tenth Earl of Eglinton decided to build a new parish village in the 1760s this way of life changed completely. Alexander Montgomery was supposedly inspired by a pretty Italian (some say Swiss) village on his European travels, but his motivations went beyond the aesthetic. Planned villages appeared all over Scotland in the 1735 to 1850 period, built by educated and monied landowners who had the power to take part in the agricultural revolution. And revolution it was; by 1790 all Eaglesham's fermtouns had gone. Runrig was abandoned and farms were enclosed, leases were extended and given to those willing to experiment with new farming methods. As a result the number of farms and tenants working them decreased dramatically; the village was built to accommodate the surplus workforce. Eaglesham population figures of the 1790s show an unexpected decrease of about 100 from the mid-century point, reflecting the uncertainty of those living there, who had to decide whether to leave for agricultural work elsewhere or try and find a niche within the new village economy.

Some effects of the – at first unsettling – new regime were surprising. When the villagers' old homes were pulled down, the tacks made available as building plots hardly seemed sufficient compensation. This didn't concern the writer of the First Statistical Account who commented approvingly on how the parishes' morals had improved along with the rising rents, hard work being 'the best preventative of vice'. The end result, however, was actually very positive for the villagers, empowering them in a new and tangible way. Few tacks were taken up in the first few years but by 1774 a Feuars Society had been formed to petition the earl about villagers' views and requirements. An important right of the Feuars was to cut peat and graze animals on an area up on the moor. The letting of this ground to local farmers produced a steady income in the time before the estate was sold by the Earl to the Gilmours. Accounts of the time state that the Feuars were under 'no servitude to their landlords' and in 1832 they were chasing John White, mill owner, for unpaid ground rent owed to them, an indication of their new-found empowerment.

What emerged over the 1760 to 1790 period was a pretty village of two main streets facing each other over a large communal green. In order to support the population, the earl allowed a cotton mill to be built at the top end of the village, thereby introducing Eaglesham to the Industrial Revolution. By 1831 the population had doubled to over 2,000, with housing in the village becoming overcrowded as a result.

Despite Eaglesham's success, the finances of the Montgomery family floundered due to the extravagance of two of Alexander's successors. The twelfth earl poured the family coffers into the ill-fated Ardrossan harbour venture, while the thirteenth spent thousands on the pointless Eglinton Tournament. After centuries of ownership by the Montgomery family, the estate was sold in 1844 to Allan and James Gilmour, the former a ship-owning merchant from Glasgow.

The Gilmours maintained the paternalistic outlook of lairds, refusing to allow a railway station at the village because it would have encouraged villa-building commuters from the city. It wasn't their wisest move. Eaglesham was made safe from the outside world, but it was hardly secure within its own, with the mills and handloom weaving industry failing and no alternatives in sight. Over the 1841 to 1861 period the population dropped steadily, and when the mill, ever susceptible to fire damage, burned down in 1876 the decision was made not to rebuild it. With no work it was just not possible for people to stay and a drift away began. By 1901 the population numbered just over 1,000, similar to the level at its foundation in the late eighteenth century. As a ghost town full of abandoned properties (many of which had been in need of renovation anyway), Eaglesham became increasingly dilapidated.

In 1926 the *Renfrewshire and Paisley Gazette* advertised the estate as being for sale again, along with the Gilmour's Fingalton estate, both of which were disposed of in lots. Despite this upheaval, Eaglesham's population revived slightly over the decade as private bus companies made the village more accessible. By 1931 there had been a 50% population rise to 1,600, with incomers encouraged by increasingly popular day trips to Eaglesham.

It must have been a shock then when a member of Renfrewshire council suggested the village should be entirely demolished in the late 1930s. Some houses were empty because of damp, whereas others were occupied by virtual squatters, but the councillor's extreme plan to deal with these problems was nipped in the bud by the start of World War II.

By the late forties two incomers (Miss K. Whyte and Mrs Davidson) had begun to stir up interest in Eaglesham's conservation. 1954 saw the start of a letter-writing campaign complaining about houses which had been boarded up or demolished under the post-war Housing Act, leaving the village scattered with gap sites. Two years later the Gazette carried an announcement advertising a world-wide appeal for funds towards Eaglesham's preservation, sponsored by the Earl of Eglinton. Just over ten years later the village became a designated Conservation Area, with a strong community spirit coming to the fore. Many incomers became involved in village life through restoration of their own houses, which in turn contributed to the preservation of a close-knit community. One of the most significant achievements over these years was the registering of the village as an A-listed site by the Secretary of State. While most buildings within it were B-listed, their conformity of style made the village itself 'A' category, the new grading ensuring that individual cottages could not be tampered with.

These days Eaglesham is an attractive village populated by commuters who also take a part in community life. In the seventies the village was the subject of a local plan by Eastwood District Council that looked into its potential development over the decade. Its concerns are still the concerns of today; how to manage the flow of freight traffic (a bypass was promised thirty years ago); when permission should be granted for new housing; and how best to preserve the original village. The 1991 census showed a healthy population of around 4,000, the highest proportion of which was in the 30-34 age group. As in the late seventies the village seems popular with young families, still, as in the 1930s, used as a day-trip destination by those wanting a drive into the country or a night in the Eglinton Arms.

The Covenanters' Monument in Eaglesham parish graveyard was erected in memory of Thomas and Robert Lockhart, outsiders who were caught and killed near the village in the 1680s. Various legends centre around nearby Lochgoin Farmhouse, which was known as a safe place for covenanters and was apparently sought out by some fleeing after the Battle of Bothwell Brig. Legend has it that Captain John Paton and his followers were being given food and shelter there by the Howie family when a party of dragoons arrived. Isabel Howie supposedly intervened to stop Sergeant Rae firing a gun at the refugees as they escaped out of the back of the house, and was driven out of her home afterwards for her trouble. Eaglesham village had its notable characters on both sides of the dispute. Sir Alexander, the sixth earl, known as Greysteele, signed the covenant in 1638. Alexander Home, on the other hand, was the unpopular Sheriff Depute, accused of persecuting covenanters in the 1680s. Tradition has it that his grave became the site of a dunghill although this seems too sweet a revenge to be true.

Eaglesham from the south. According to the writer of the First Statistical Account in the 1790s, Eaglesham was named after the majestic birds of prey which once inhabited the district's woods. Fifty years later, Rev. William Colville, writer of the second account, was unimpressed with his predecessor's explanation. He considered it 'utterly unfounded [and] . . . a vulgar mistake' since the indigenous golden eagle preferred the wide open spaces of the mountains. The eagle was used by the village as a romantic emblem regardless, appearing on the Feuars' flag and as a decoration for the parish church. The original church was, in fact, a more likely influence on the village's name. A compound of the Celtic *eagles* (meaning church) and the Saxon *ham* (hamlet or village) was a fitting description of the old Kirkton village radiating from the church.

Montgomery Square, Eaglesham

Eaglesham belonged to the Montgomery family for at least six centuries. Under the feudal system land was acquired either through good relations with those in power (whether the monarchy or another feudal lord) or tactical marriages. Records show that Eaglesham was initially in the possession of the Stewart family after it was gifted by David I to his steward Walter Stewart. Stewart passed the lands on to his friend Roger de Montgomerie as a dowry for his daughter Margery whom de Montgomerie married. The French knight had come to Britain in 1068 after William the Conqueror's victory at the Battle of Hastings. Later, in 1360, Sir John de Montgomerie married Elizabeth, daughter of Sir Hugh de Eglinton, picking up the baronies of Eglinton and Ardrossan along the way. He also managed to acquire the family the Earl of Eglinton title as a reward for supporting the future King James IV in the feud against his father.

Montgomery Square, running from Strathaven Road to the lane at the Cross Keys Inn, was the heart of old Eaglesham village. The lanes between its houses and yards led to the old fermtouns, farms, peat cuttings and muir as well as to nearby settlements such as Strathaven, Darvel and Newmilns. The road to Darvel was also crossed by the Kilmarnock and Glasgow roads, and this concentration of important routes led some to believe that Montgomery Square was on the site of the mid-eighteenth century Main Street. In the past Montgomery Street was known simply as South Street and Polnoon Street as North Street. Parts of Montgomery Street show evidence of its late eighteenth century origins, when the new Eaglesham village was being built. No. 66 has the date 1797 carved on its lintel, and no. 50 is inscribed 'James Kego and Jean Mitchell 1774'.

Sculptor Work by the late Wm. Gemmell, Eaglesham.

MONTGOMERY ST EAGLESHAM

This stretch of Montgomery Street includes the Pillar House in whose outhouses the family of William Gemmell, local joiner and sculptor, stored his creations. Most of his work was either connected with Robert Burns, or Glasgow characters who visited the village regularly. Eastwood District Council bought the remaining examples as one of its last acts as council of the area, and the building is being converted into a heritage centre. Alexander Montgomery, who decided to demolish and rebuild Eaglesham, never got the chance to see the finished village. He was shot dead by Mungo Campbell, a trespasser and known poacher whom he challenged on his Ayrshire estate. There was a long-standing feud between the two men, Campbell having threatened the earl with a gun before. Campbell committed suicide before he could be hanged and was buried at Salisbury Crags in Edinburgh. Perhaps to prove that he was actually dead (there were rumours that he had escaped) an Edinburgh mob dug him up again; friends later buried him at sea to prevent further desecrations.

The agricultural revolution brought significant improvements in farming methods, and Eaglesham grew as a result of these. In the Middle Ages agriculture revolved around the rearing of cattle and sheep and the growing of oats. The runrig system meant that land that would later comprise a single farm was divided between many tenants, each of whom were allocated a small strip raised into a ridge a couple of feet high. These tenants lived in collections of farm buildings housing their animals as well as their families, the dunghills right outside the front door. An inefficient infield/outfield system was used whereby the infield (nearest to the farmhouse and occupying 30-50% of the land) was cultivated and the outfield was used as pasture. Even in the late seventeenth century runrig was still in favour with some landlords because it increased the number of people on their land, manpower being an major indication of status under the feudal system.

MONTGOMERY ST. EAGLESHAM

The shop on the right has gone, the building probably converted into a home. Motivation for agricultural change came from landlords keen to increase their profits. Runrig wasn't particularly effective because leases were short-term and it relied on co-operation amongst tenants, who had to share tools and other resources. To improve the situation larger farms were leased to individuals who introduced new crops such as turnip and potatoes (potatoes were actually mistrusted by some husbandmen, who believed they soured the land). Land was enclosed by hedges to provide shelter and protection from animals, making the herd-boy redundant at the same time. The result was fewer farms with displaced workers becoming tradesmen or weavers in the villages. Eaglesham's Market Act of 1672 made it possible to make a living selling goods at its weekly and annual markets.

Montgomery Street, Townhead. Although few villages of its age have survived so intact, the model on which Eaglesham was built was typical of the 'improving' culture of the times; rather than being a homage to a European town, it was actually very much to do with changes in Scotland. Although the 'agricultural revolution' did not gain momentum until the 1780s, John Cockburn was beginning to carve his reputation as an agricultural reformer as early as 1714. He inherited lands at Ormiston in that year and immediately set about improving them, introducing enclosure and nineteen year leases, rebuilding his local fermtoun and sending his tenants endless letters of advice. As one of the first improvers he was a big influence on many landowners and Alexander Montgomery consulted Ormiston tenants during the building of the new Eaglesham. In 1720 an Honourable Society of Improvers was set up in Edinburgh to promote the movement. Its members didn't need to make money and were principally motivated by patriotism, doing their bit to bring Scotland into the modern age.

When the village was developed, tacks on the site of the old kirkton were offered on 999 year terms, not feus at all despite the villagers calling themselves feuars. Those who didn't have cash to buy a tack could rent one from a tacksman. However you got hold of one, a house had to be built on it within five years or you were fined five pounds, the equivalent of eight to ten years rent; the last resort was eviction. The deal between the earl and his feuars was complicated and involved concessions and co-operation on both sides. Houses were built to strict instructions as to height and width, but materials such as stone and sand could be taken from the estate. The orry had to be evened out and prepared for grass by the villagers, but they were allowed to sow and reap one crop of grain on it as compensation. When Eaglesham's Conservation Plan got started one of its first aims was to get the electricity lines in this picture moved underground, as they were deemed to spoil the character of the village.

Eaglesham's tacks or feus are still valid, although over the years they have been transferred to its various owners, latterly Renfrewshire County Council. At one time an individual in the village made an effort to buy up a lot of feus, causing some concern as to their motives, although nothing came of the plan. No doubt the imposing Feuars Society would have had something to say about it had it gone ahead. The society (confined to the lower part of the village) still has meetings today; in earlier times those attending got a pie and a cup of tea paid for with money raised from those fined for non-attendance.

Initially, Eaglesham had few decent services. It was too far away from Glasgow, its market town, and good coal was at least seven miles distant. The nearest magistrate was four miles away, given by one eighteenth century commentator as the reason for the village being constantly 'oppressed by gangs of gypsies'. The Feuars had grazing rights on seventy acres of land up on the moor, part of which they let out as farmland to raise money for facilities to improve village life. Street lighting was paid for in this way as was subscription to Glasgow hospitals, although improvements weren't always to the villagers' advantage. The introduction of steam power and gas lighting in mills, for example, often resulted in longer working hours. In 1777 the Feuars agreed to finance a service which seems positively masochistic today – paying one shilling each a year for the privilege of having a piper wake them at 6.30 a.m. each day – although there is no evidence that the piper's services were actually provided.

MONTGOMERY ST. EAGLESHAM
FROM U.F. CHURCH

By the 1970s Montgomery Street was being used as a passageway by lorries carrying heavy loads from the Central Belt to the steel-making areas. Traffic had been a problem since the forties and was mentioned specifically in the Abercrombie Report in 1949. There are still plans for a bypass, for completion by 2003, but villagers think it is unlikely to happen since it's not believed to be a priority for the new council. What may be built instead is a Glasgow 'southern orbital route', travelling from East Kilbride around the village to Newton Mearns, following the line of the Humbie Road. Any improvement at all would be welcomed by those living in Montgomery Street since their homes would increase in value as a result.

Kirkstyle, dating back to the seventeenth century and the oldest building in the village, lies behind the small buildings on the left-hand corner. It was saved from demolition because it was set back from the line of the street.

Polnoon Street was named after Polnoon Castle, built on the banks of the River Cart and rumoured to have the usual secret passage leading out to a nearby burn. In 1388 Sir John de Montgomerie took Henry Percy (known as Hotspur) prisoner at the Battle of Otterburn and supposedly built the castle with his ransom (poind) money. Although its walls were eight feet thick there were only ruins left by the time the Second Statistical Account was written in the 1840s. Rev. Colville stated that it was only possible to learn about it from books at that time because so little of it was left, commenting rather over-dramatically that 'The illiterate now despise or overlook it'. The literate certainly didn't take too much care with its history since Sir Walter Scott placed it in Ayrshire in his *Minstrelsy* and *Tales of a Grandfather*.

The house on the left, at the top of Polnoon Street, was known as 'Hillhead' and was once the last house in the village before the fields.

Polnoon Street. The Montgomerys had a long-standing feud with the Cunninghams which began after James II granted the former family the office of the Bailiery of Cunninghame. Incidents between the two families became increasingly violent, also involving some branches of the Kennedy family. In the late 1480s Hugh, the third Montgomery earl, raided the Cunningham residence of Kirrielaw near Stevenston. Forty years later the Cunninghams burned down Eglinton Castle (along with all the family charters and papers) and even by the 1580s feelings ran high enough for them to shoot dead Hugh, the fourth earl, near Stewarton.

Eaglesham's twelfth earl takes the dubious credit for landing the Montgomery family in financial disaster; in fact, he took all the credit available at the time with the result that Eaglesham was put on the market in 1835. He invested in a giant harbour on the Ardrossan estate (large enough to hold 100 ships) and a canal to connect it to Glasgow, an act of Parliament approving the scheme in 1806. Despite setbacks, the earl continued to pour both his own and borrowed funds into the project in an attempt to complete it. He died in 1819, leaving the estate to a five-year-old grandson who proved to have weaknesses of his own once he came of age.

Polnoon Street. The thirteenth earl spent an incredible £40,000 on the Eglinton Tournament, which took place in 1839. Medieval tournaments were fashionable at the time, inspired mainly by Sir Walter Scott, although the earl was supposedly influenced by his step-family. Two years were spent organising accommodation, entertainment, costumes and food for an event which was ruined by rain (and characterised by distinctly modern umbrellas) on the day. Even before it took place it was obvious that the Eaglesham estate was not going to remain intact. An act of Parliament had been passed five years earlier releasing the earl from the conditions of his predecessor's will which prevented him from selling parts of the estate. The tournament didn't cause the Montgomeries' financial ruin, but it certainly exacerbated it, and all to prove that 'the age of chivalry wasn't dead'. It's a pity this particular earl didn't make do with doffing his cap at gentlewomen and helping a few old folk across the road.

The male Montgomery line came to an end in 1612 when the fifth earl died without heirs. Before his death he obtained a crown charter to name an heir in the female line and chose his aunt's youngest son, Sir Alexander Seton. Seton took on the privileges and estates in return for changing his name to Montgomerie. (At this point Montgomery became Montgomerie to signify this historical event). Ever canny, when the Seton line became extinct 150 years later, the Montgomeries claimed their lands.

This picture was taken at the meeting point between Montgomery and Polnoon Streets. Eaglesham had to import coal from Glasgow, Wellshot and Hamilton since its own natural resources were of minimal practical use. The First Statistical Account states that two miles away at Ballagioch Hill there was a certain type of red stone which signified the presence of silver and lead in the parish. There was also a volcanic stone (Osmond Stone), prized for its ability to withstand high temperatures. This was used as a base for bakers' ovens and in fireplaces but its popularity faded in the mid-nineteenth century since its variable density meant that some bread in a bakers' batch would be burned before the rest of it was cooked. A quarry 'on the roadside to Glasgow' was mentioned around the same time as containing various minerals such as jasper and blue quartz. Sphagnum moss (one of the components of peat) was gathered by Eaglesham women during World War II for use in dressings, although no reason is given why it was used for this.

In the past Eaglesham's location on land riddled with springs caused health problems. Homes became extremely damp and could be improved only by raising the floors or building drains, both of which were expensive measures. One historian wrote that 'Consumptions are not uncommon; but most deaths are occasioned by fevers'. Smallpox was common and killed many children, despite the development of inoculations. Parents were suspicious of the process whereby a healthy child was infected with the disease thinking they might, '[bring] trouble on their children . . . by their own hands'. It's easy to smile at this but our own reaction to modern diseases such as AIDS shows similar ignorance. Certainly, early English experiments with inoculation used a primitive lancet and resulted in a few cases of smallpox. Asides from a mistrust of medicine, however, there were also deep-rooted religious and cultural prejudices. A central aspect of Calvinism was a belief in pre-destination; attempts to tamper with one's fate in any way were considered as an act against divine providence.

Polnoon Street, Eaglesham.

By the time of the Second Statistical Account, smallpox had returned with 'fearful frequency' but its writer claimed the symptoms were different and seldom claimed lives, although no explanation is offered for this. Medical understanding was still primitive, and at the time a form of wad impregnated with arsenic was being produced at Millhall; users were reminded not to place it on an open wound. By 1865 the Compulsory Vaccination Act was in place, meaning that children had to be registered for inoculation within six months of their birth. In Eaglesham the Registrar was James B. Yuille who was also the local schoolmaster. After the six month period had passed Yuille had one month in which to chase offending families up, requiring a certificate from them saying that inoculation had taken place within ten days of despatch of the notice. If this wasn't provided the family were fined twenty shillings (plus an extra one shilling which went to Yuille) and if this wasn't paid the parents could then be imprisoned for ten days.

A look at some of the nineteenth-century inscriptions in Eaglesham kirkyard reveals the vulnerability of human life at the time. Of Robert Brierton and Barbara Montgomerie's five children, four died within a five year period in the 1860s. Only one of Robert Arneil and Janet Craig's children made it beyond their early twenties. Despite the absence of a railway at Eaglesham their son Robert was killed (presumably by a train) at Blantyre Station in 1874, aged twenty-four. Five of Peter McFarlane and Elizabeth Currie's children died before the age of ten, their longest-living child dying at the relatively young age of fifty-five. Again, only one of John Paton and Janet Gilmour's eight children made it past their mid-twenties. They lost two infants within a few of years of each other, baby John dying in 1832 aged one, and his sister Mary surviving only nineteen hours following her birth three years later.

During the mid-nineteenth century Eaglesham became quite cosmopolitan as labourers arrived from Ireland and the Highlands to work at the mills or on local farms. By 1851 50% of Eaglesham's farmers were recent incomers. The Irish (trying to escape poverty in their own country) were reputed to be 'contained' in Paddy's Castle in Montgomery Street but by the mid-nineteenth century they lived throughout the village. Eaglesham was known for its lack of poverty, at least in historical accounts dating from the late 1700s to the mid-1800s. A historian of the 1790s stated that Eaglesham's inhabitants were industrious and comfortable and that 'no parish has fewer real poor'. At that time the charity roll was seldom above seven people and, although some families needed help, an assessment (appeal to the congregation and heritors) was felt unnecessary. Later years saw the establishment of Burial and Penny Societies to save towards the costs of burial and sickness.

One of the houses set back from Cheapside Road is a miniature of Polnoon Lodge and was once occupied by the estate factor. Eaglesham Bowling Greens are nearby.

THE BOWLING GREEN, EAGLESHAM.

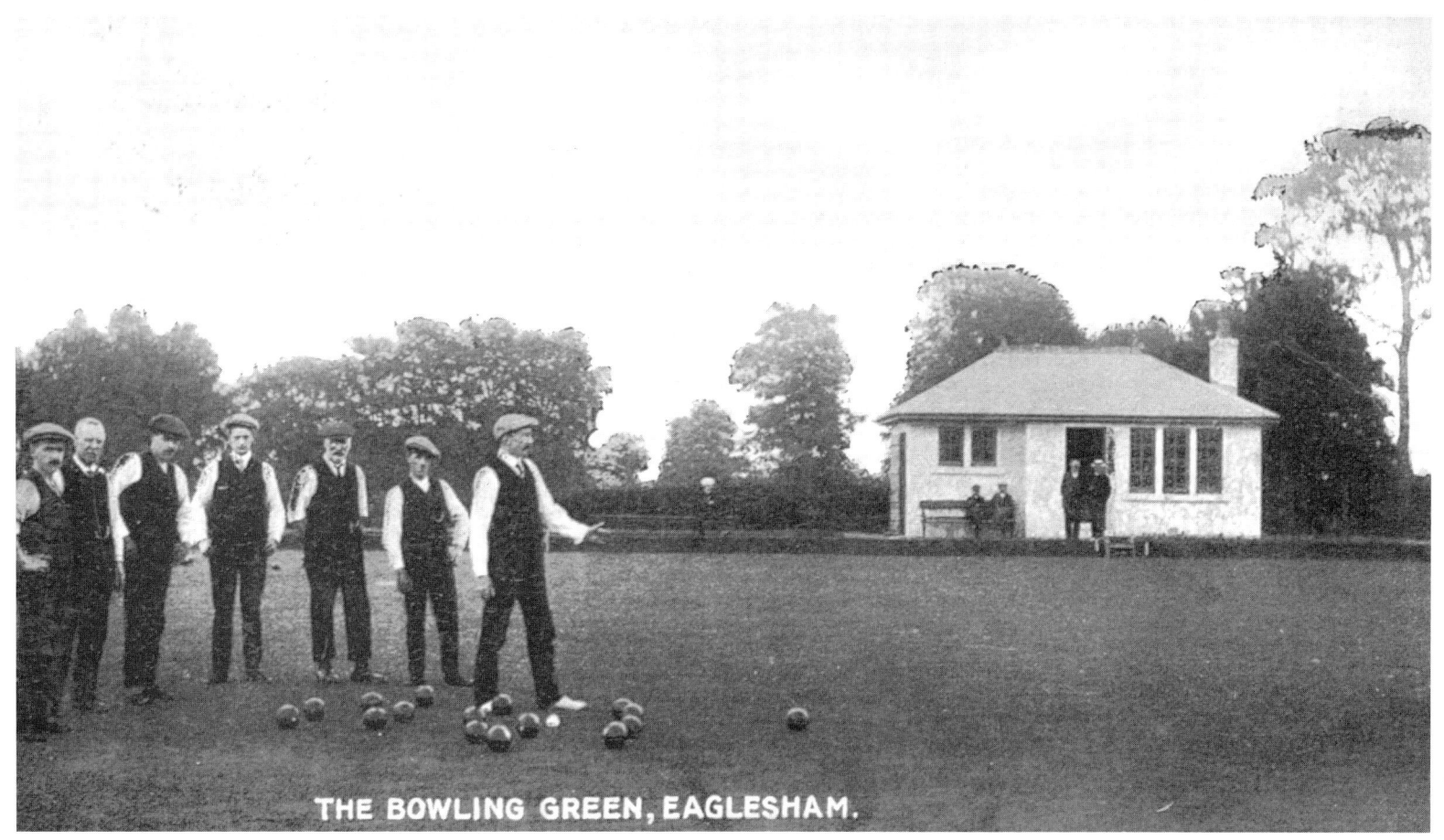

Eaglesham's bowling green still exists, tucked behind the Cheapside houses, although it now has a new pavilion and adjacent tennis courts. The village has enjoyed various recreations over the centuries. In the 1790s there were eighteen pubs which the writer of the First Statistical Account assured us were having 'a very bad effect' on the population of the comparatively small parish. By the 1890s the Kirk Session had banned alcohol at all further ordinations, although this can be put down more to Victorian puritanism than Eaglesham villagers' particular excesses. In terms of sport, curling was popular by the mid-nineteenth century (because of all the lochs and reservoirs), as was quoiting. Poaching was also mentioned as a common pastime not of the country people but by those in the village who were 'bad sitters at the loom'. As ever, the upper classes had grander sports. The Earl of Eglinton and The Marquis of Douglas were both involved in the Clydesdale Coursing Society which managed the parish's wild hare, 'an object worthy of pursuit' because of its reputed strength and hardiness.

CHEAPSIDE EAGLESHAM.

Eaglesham had a streak of eccentric radicalism in its past, not least in its earls. While the twelfth had his failed harbour and the thirteenth his grandiose tournament, the eighth earl chose a ninety-year-old bride. This aristocratic eccentricity was reflected in certain parish inhabitants. Some of Eaglesham's farmers, particularly Paterson of Stonebyres and Wodraw of Hill Farm, were well-known for their antisocial behaviour. A serious fracas occurred in 1725 when some farm servants from Mearns wandered on to the wrong land by mistake when collecting rushes, and were attacked by labourers. Collectively the villagers ran their potential new minister, Thomas Clark, out of town, when his ordination was attempted in 1765. The new village farming system of the latter part of the century had a civilising influence on the area, since the new tenants were more interested in improving their harvest than defending territorial rights. Still, political radicalism survived amongst the weavers and the Reform Act of 1832 was celebrated by their setting a cart-load of coal alight at the village cross roads.

Just what Eaglesham villagers had against Thomas Clark is unclear in the accounts of the time, although their feelings were plain. A year after the Earl of Eglinton had him put forward as the parish minister only one person had signed his call to office and it took the help of a group of soldiers to get him safely ordained. Despite the feelings of his parishioners he stayed in the job until his death in 1783. He was described by some as a man 'of learning and ability' (he had been librarian of Glasgow University) but resentment continued to simmer against him and he certainly managed to blot his copy book during his term of office. In the mid-1770s the Moderator of the Presbytery called a meeting after Clark let slip to a colleague that he was 'irregularly married' to one Peggy Wilson. A minister from Irvine gave proof that a marriage had taken place although there was no marriage certificate. During his three month suspension the villagers petitioned the Presbytery about his bad conduct but he was reinstated.

Gilmour Street, Coronation Buildings, Eaglesham

This picture shows the old school house, Coronation Buildings, the Eglinton Arms Hotel and, beyond the orry, the buildings at the end of Polnoon Street. In the 1930s many houses in the village suffered from damp. Some people didn't pay rent and were technically squatters. By the end of the decade the outlook was so bad that there were suggestions that the entire village should be pulled down. This was unpopular and is touted today as the opinion of a Philistine, but was really no different from Alexander Montgomery's 'out with the old, in with the new' viewpoint of the 1700s. Instead, the village was saved by the start of World War II which meant that more pressing concerns were given precedence. Eaglesham became an evacuee village and women made up scarves and gloves and assembled helmets for soldiers as part of the war effort. There was a bandage-making class and the Women's Voluntary Service ran a rest centre for victims of the Clydebank Blitz and the Greenock bombings.

One of the strangest events of World War II involved Rudolph Hess (Hitler's deputy) crashing his plane at Floors Farm in Eaglesham. Hess was apparently on a personal mission to end the war and had mistaken nearby Eaglesham House for the Duke of Hamilton's residence. He knew the Duke socially, and overestimated the influence he wielded to the extent that he thought Hamilton could intervene to end the war. During the thirties many high-profile Germans developed a fascination for the British aristocracy, admiring their country house lifestyle and what they considered to be their refined tastes. Hess was discovered in a field by David McLean, an Eaglesham ploughman, who was regaled as a hero by the sensationalist press, although his only claims were that he had helped Hess back to his house and made him a cup of tea. Hess's mistake resulted in him being held captive from 1941 until his death in 1987.

THE CROSS EAGLESHAM

The papers preferred their own version of the story, however, which was that McLean had captured Hess in yokel fashion, at the end of a pitchfork. A brand new (and doctored) pitchfork was acquired and despatched to America where it raised some £9,000 for the war effort. Later, it was honoured with a place in a museum of war relics. Hess himself was eventually removed from the farm by the Home Guard and became the last person to be imprisoned in the Tower of London. He was convicted at the Nuremberg trials after the war and locked up for the rest of his life. Following his transfer to Germany, 100 soldiers were sent by the allies to guard his prison and, when he died at the age of ninety-three after almost half a century of solitary confinement, it was apparently at his own hand.

Gilmour Street, with the Eglinton Arms on the right. Eaglesham's first official public transport was a horse-drawn bus which connected the village to Clarkston railway station. This was later replaced by the Caledonian Motor Car Service which connected the village to Cathcart station as well. In the twenties private bus companies made Eaglesham less isolated, the population rising by 500 over the 1911 to 1930 period.

The Caledonian Railway charabanc at Clarkston Station. This service ran between 1906 and 1908, and the bus was a Durham-Churchill, manufactured in Sheffield.

Sanderson Bros. of Glasgow ran this AEC bus between Eaglesham, Clarkston and Glasgow in the mid-1920s. The picture was taken at the bus stance in Clyde Street, Glasgow, where all services to the south of the city left from at the time.

Coronation Buildings, the Glasgow-style tenement block beyond the Eglinton Arms, was one of the few buildings to be demolished as part of Eaglesham's conservation programme. The tenement was considered out of keeping with the village's character. Other buildings had been spoilt by adverts, signs or inappropriate twentieth century street furniture. Gap sites were also a problem, the Royal Oak Hotel (next to the Cross Keys), for example, being demolished to make space for a garage which was never built. Further setbacks included alterations made to homes at a time when council approval wasn't necessary, and the colours owners painted their houses even at a time when it was. An early opinion of the Eaglesham Preservation Society was that buildings could be painted 'any colour . . . with the exception of green' but this *laissez-faire* attitude changed as houses in the village began to emerge in a rainbow of – sometimes sickly – colours.

Gilmour Street, with Montgomery Square leading off to the right. The distinctive building on the corner was later rebuilt in the 'village style'. Morale-raising efforts of the First World War were just as eccentric as the 'Hess at the end of a pitchfork' stories of the 1940s. The *Paisley and Renfrewshire Gazette* of 1919 stated that the National Egg Collection had so far collected 41 million eggs for distribution to soldiers overseas, although exactly how they were to get to their destination unbroken wasn't mentioned. On a more serious subject, advertisements appeared at the end of the war referring to the 'discharged serviceman's badge'. This badge, the ads claimed, testified that the wearer had benefited from training and discipline, was capable of machine-like time-keeping and could show proper respect to his superiors. It seems a rather lame measure to give ex-soldiers kudos on civvie street, and of little benefit during the depression of the twenties and thirties.

Both the stretch of shops on the left and the large building on the right have been converted into houses; the latter held a grocers, post office and butchers at one point.

POLNOON LODGE
PHONE 11.
EAGLESHAM.

Polnoon Lodge dates back to the early eighteenth century and was one of the original landmarks (together with the churchyard and Kirkstyle) which had to be negotiated in planning the new village. The lodge was built as a hunting residence by the ninth earl and used only for a few weeks each year, which perhaps accounts for the fact that it was in need of renovation in the 1790s. Situated on the north-east side of Gilmour Street, it took its name from Polnoon Castle, itself in a state of ruins at the time of its namesake's construction. The lodge became the home of James Gilmour for fifteen years after he and his brother bought Eaglesham Estate in the 1840s. By the late 1920s it had been reinvented once again as a temperance hotel, although a few decades later it lay abandoned. The lodge's most recent restoration was completed by Renfrew County Council who developed it into award-winning housing for the elderly. The library and public halls on Gilmour Street stand on the original site of its stables and coach house.

Picket Loch. Eaglesham.

Picket Loch was named after the pickets posted by covenanters to watch for enemies during their secret meetings (conventicles) on the moors. By the 1840s over 200 acres of Eaglesham land was covered in reservoirs, supplying mills at Eaglesham, Busby and Fenwick. The series of reservoirs still exists today. A new water processing plant was opened about a year ago, although the reservoirs are now valued as much for their trout fishing as a water supply. Other natural energy sources are tapped into at the wind farm on Fenwick Moor.

Eaglesham House was built by the Gilmours as a residence in the late 1850s. As with many large country houses it was eventually abandoned, and remained unoccupied until the Polish army acquired it as a transport depot during World War II. After the war its industrial status continued when it became a grass drying factory. In 1954 300 tons of grass caught fire on the ground floor, with firemen from Darnley, Paisley and Glasgow battling to stop the blaze reaching the north side where 200 gallons of petrol were stored. Despite their efforts, Eaglesham House was completely destroyed. In the early eighties Linn Products applied to build a factory on the site. The area had originally been 'green belt', and there were many local objections, but the Scottish Office granted permission in 1984 because of the employment opportunities. Linn's owner, Mr Tiefenbrun, entrusted architect Richard Rogers to design a plant which wouldn't disrupt the landscape, although Rogers' more famous creation, the Pompidou Arts Centre in Paris, is hardly low-key.

Eaglesham Old School, on Strathaven Road, is still in use today as a primary school. Its frontage is recognisable from this shot, although the building itself has been considerably extended. The old school took over from its predecessor further down the road at the cross. In the mid-nineteenth century Eaglesham's parish school stood in Gilmour Street. It was run by Mr Smellie and had ninety pupils. In addition to this there were three private schools including the Female Industrial School. At the time schoolmasters boarded on the corner of Montgomery Street and Gilmour Street.

OLD MILL EAGLESHAM

Following the establishment of two mills, one at the orry and one on the Millhall estate, Eaglesham flourished. Pubs, schools, library and post office all appeared during a time when the villagers had ample employment whether as weavers or mill workers. The orry mill had various owners but was under the control of Maclean and Brodie of Glasgow by the 1840s. Well over 50% of its 200 employees were under the age of twenty, children being sought-after in this line of work because their size meant they were nimble and could negotiate the machinery more easily. The orry mill burned down more than once, and this susceptibility to fire was cited by Crawfurd and Robertson in their *History of Renfrewshire* as the reason Eaglesham hadn't become one of the 'hotbeds of vice and forerunners of a dissolution of manner' which they labelled all other mill towns as. The vice was blamed on the large numbers of uneducated young people working together and the fires at Eaglesham, despite being industrial disasters, were credited with nipping this trend in the bud.

THE OLD MILL, EAGLESHAM.

Millhall's mill was eventually taken over by Ludovick Gavin who bought it from the previous owner's creditors. He was reputed to have had a mill at the top of Montgomery Street but this seems to be unfounded, although he may have worked in the village. His business concentrated on producing shuttle cards for powerlooms and candle-wicks, although it was a smaller concern than its orry rival, operating on half the 50 hp it used. Nevertheless the orry mill was hardly at the forefront of technology, and was originally confined to mule-spinning with no powerlooms. Following the establishment of the village mill in the early 1790s Eaglesham's population increased four-fold, although the incomers weren't always welcomed by the original villagers. The Feuars Society showed this clearly by banning all of those who occupied the new mill houses from their ranks, a rule still in force today.

Mid Road cuts across the village 'orry'. The orry mill burned down for a second time in the 1870s, and as the disaster followed a serious decline in both the cotton and handloom weaving industries it was not rebuilt. From a high of around 400 weavers, the village's workforce had dropped to just over 100, and with at least half of those over fifty years of age the industry was obviously dying. Millhall had attempted to keep up with technology by installing powerlooms (after Gavin's death) for weaving blankets, but these and other improvements, such as the carding machine installed at the orry in 1871, reduced the need for human labour. Besides, the industry was floundering because of cheap imports and the difficulty of keeping up with technology. After the fire Eaglesham was left without the industry it had depended on for a century. With their reason for living there gone the mill workers began to drift away, their homes left empty.

Today nothing is left of the orry mill above ground level, although it is still possible to make out its foundations. When the mill closed it lay empty for a time and was mostly used as a playground by local children, although an old man was allowed to keep pigs and cattle in one of its buildings by the Feuars. The cattle had to be taken away to the fields behind it every day on account of the ancient ban on using the orry for grazing. In the 1870s the Gilmours allowed stones from some of the buildings to be used to build the dry stane wall which leaves the village in the direction of Eaglesham House. This project was aimed at helping Eaglesham's unemployed weavers and mill workers but was a very temporary sticking plaster.